The χ Point

Hugo Jepsen

Preface

A relationship! Can a relationship save you? A lot of people say that it doesn't; but what if it can save you?

Someone who is completely wholesome falls in love with someone who is completely broken - *'The X Point'*.

The story of this poetry book follows two people with two different perspectives on relationships; one who wants to make sure that everything improves in a positive light and that everything stays healthy and stable with a logical way of thinking versus someone who tries their best to be conscious and healthy while struggling with depression and internal trauma of relationships.

Enjoy!

Chapters:

holding you in the future

I never get to hold you
as long as I want to —
time passes by quickly
when we both never do.

Until I see you standing
in the midst of my thunderstorm,
I'm fine with staying in your arms.

If nobody ever understands
when you speak about love —
I hope to make sure that
what you speak is enough.

I never get to hold you tight,
but someday, in the future,
I hope to hold you as mine.

green branches

The green branches of olive trees
are growing themselves to
pierce their roots inside of me —
What am I supposed to do?

The semblance of the shade
and the yearning they utterly make
and the gripping sound
that I hear whenever they break.

And they've broken out
inside a body that is mine —
all the words they tell me about
are about tipping points in time.

They've pierced through
and we've become one —
the way that I feel the world
is the way that we've become —
and baby, it burns, I feel it burn.

peaceful places

Heartstrings playing songs -
I've been on roadblocks,
how God knows for how long.

It craves your touch,
so close to your soul -
is it real or is it in my head?
is it fear of being in love?

People who don't have a home
fear that they may be left alone.
But in loneliness, a peaceful place,
or something like that I've thought so.

Is it right? Am I doing the right thing?
As if all my feathers dropped one by one,
and once called an angel who has lost his wings.

written all over your face

I'm out of my head,
it's sinking inside of me,
but whenever you're ready,
I know that I will be - I will be.

I'm out of my vest -
a war inside of my eyes -
what I can see clearly
is me in your arms tonight.

As long as you feel it too,
I know that I will be safe -
it's written all over your face.

every time I'm with you

I feel you as a whole on me
when you're not even there -
tell me if ever love has been fair.

Every time I'm with you,
I forget all I've ever known -
every time you tell me to come,
I go places I'd never go alone.

We can face the danger
for tonight and forget -
hope that you never
think that I was a mistake.

And every time you feel pain,
I hope to be there to
burn your tears away.

for all these years

When I was not able
to feel nothing at all -
You came in as stable
in the midst of my downfall.

With all things to
be grateful for -
is being in love with you
what I'm grateful for the most.

And late at night, I think -
thinking about all my fears,
and how I'm holding on -
my sadness became happy tears
and since I've been alone all these years,
and now that I'm not - well, cheers!

assumptions of love

Soaking up in tears —
if I'm mistaken, I apologize
but there's something in your eyes
that got my heart hypnotized.

All these assumptions made -
going too fast, going too slow -
and if I cared just a little,
that's not what I feel in my soul.

And alone - glistening in the rain -
all these flowers growing up on the roof.
If I could climb the ladder to get them,
I'd pick them up to decorate your room.

If that's not enough - What is then?
If that's not love - How do you know?
What do people say? - Are they happy then?
I don't think I know, I do not think so.

I just know how I feel

The smell of the fish in the sea -
somewhat agonizing but refreshing -
that's the lenses which you see through me.

Antagonizing - summer strikes -
one blow of wind at a time,
and every time it gets violent,
it violates my state of mind.

If I could change, I would,
it's not in my nature
to not be at peace -
I rather just leave.

It's penetrating my soul,
knots filled with thorns,
pain is all I've ever known.

You ask me for love in return,
I'd give you so if I could
but I don't know how to -
I just know that I'm in love with you.

stay pretty, stay silent

Stay pretty, stay silent,
don't say literally, a thing -
words create arrogance.

If strength is shown,
you might lose it all
without having known.

Remain still, remain casual -
if you show that you need love,
what was sweet becomes salt.

You need to play fantasy -
life is a game, love is a game -
you've signed up for all of this;
he even gave you a nickname.

ignorance doesn't stop falling

Come in, come with everything -
consume me, possess me
since I'm trying to be all yours -
but what if I could never be?

Pointless is to touch one's heart,
scatter it all, trying to save it all -
but what if I need no saving
at the precipice of my downfall?

However - incandescent glow,
golden pages can turn mould -
such as when errors are found
when love is made to grow cold.

It is potency - the wind blows -
it's not that I don't feel pain,
just is that it became comfortable
to stop fighting against it anyway.

When the rain starts to fall,
I let it fall, I feel every drop -
I never knew how to make
my ignorant behaviour to stop.

it's ending, it's fine (interlude)

As if I could touch the sky
with both of my eyes -
as if I could just breathe
inside of me with peace.

But it's now how it goes —
flavours of insecurities
is all I've ever known.

And you've seen the best,
and you've seen the worst -
are you sure you love me?
Are you? Are you sure?

It's ending, it's fine,
it's not like I'm not sad
but I learned that it's life -
the X point in time.

painfully alive

I've never been alive,
always lived in my head.
Safer to see through my lenses,
drunk or high or the same as dead.

I am back to see my friends —
let's hit the dirty streets
while the full moon shines over it
because the night belongs to me.

Born to want to feel pleasure
but I've been staying for the pain,
I don't carry much work experience
but rumours were attributed to my name.

Mother said I work against God's will,
but that's now how He makes me feel.
And I hate to admit that I'm right
because I'm never sure of something in life.

selfish I am

Say to me you love me,
selfish I am all the time
but deep within,
I know I cross your mind.

And if you decide to come,
I'm sure that I will run
because I can't understand
how to be loved by a man.

The scent of your cologne
is stinking in my clothes
and your pain has become
a token to my oath.

When I was young,
I was pretty and free,
but things have changed
and I'm no longer who I used to be.

pale skin

Cold hands of mine,
eerie sounds I make -
what's in my mind?

Going ablaze for it all
for reasons unknown
since freezing waters
is what I've always drunk.

A path that leads me astray,
stubborn in my behaviour,
wanting things my way.

Pretty in your eyes,
attractive to your body,
barely do you know I hate what's mine.

unknown tenderness

A monster in your bed
is what I think I am -
a hunter of hearts
coming for me again.

Little stars twinkling
at the back of your wall
is my telepathy
trying to give you a call.

Please, wake up,
we need to talk
about this love.

Don't make me wait
because while I do so,
my blood grows cold
my emotions get easily sold.

sinking in confusion

We've gathered here
to be crossing lines -
if destiny has the answer,
I'd give up my own life.

Somewhat, it's empathy
to run carefree with grace -
yet, you're so eager to make me stop,
it's like your hate for me ran out of place.

You've got a knack for ghosting
while giving me ghostly dreams -
as you write my name in your body,
I feel the dirt in my mouth as if you were burying me.

I didn't have the right answer for you,
so you sink me in deep confusion -
as if I didn't have it in myself to sink in it too.

shades of lipstick

Shades of lipstick in your tie,
ten colours of the lie I was told to -
I got mistaken for the smell of blood,
but you know, I'd never be with anyone but you.

You have looked for me in others
when I was dreaming of us together -
and everything would feel like a fairytale
but the pain of losing a life is that love isn't fair.

How have I tried to end all of what I feel?
Taking the blame, taking responsibility -
trying to be an honest man but the wild side
pulls me stronger than what I'd like it to be.

Shades of lipstick is blood spilt -
who did you kill if it wasn't me?

my sadness has become beautiful

When tears are running down,
I have found no ways to stop it -
it's from tears that I'm all about.

I held your hand, too strong, I think,
I find the pain to become quite beautiful,
but I don't think you share the same feeling.

And when my tears run over you,
you make it all about bad luck
instead of taking responsibility for the things you do.

Yet, I held your hand way too strong,
I think I didn't tell you that I was scared,
but I just wanted to keep me inside your chest.

you've been changing but it's not enough

You said you can do it all night,
said that I was walking out of line,
but I can't make any excuses for you,
and for you, I can't put my trauma to the side.

Had me feeling like I've died,
I've never seen a man cry
like when I saw myself do, so,
and the fault is yours - you know?

And I see, you've been changing,
trying to be more of my taste.
And I see, you've been chasing,
but I think now it's far too late.

And you know, you messed me up,
we'll never be friends like this,
hating me, won't make me love,
wanting me, it's nothing special,
exes like you and me don't become sexual.

let's move on for a happy ending

My world has changed,
my face doesn't look the same,
but when I look into your eyes,
I still feel the same way when I was alive.

But this love has finally passed away -
you got me but I got in the way.
He makes me feel like I should
but I would love you still if I could.

He does know all the reasons
for when I cry at night
and that's comforting nonetheless -
getting better at finding happiness.

Perhaps, I'm lying to myself
and all is happening as you said -
but it's time for you to move on
and hope that happiness never ends.

Credits

Writer: Hugo Jepsen
Editor: Hugo Jepsen
Cover Creator: Hugo Jepsen
Image License: Unsplash
Publisher: Amazon

Disclaimer

Any resemblance to other creative projects is mere coincidence.

Copyrights

Protected and Licensed with a Copyright Infringement.